Extreme Nature!

Q&A

Smithsonian | Collins

An Imprint of HarperCollinsPublishers

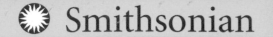 **Smithsonian**

Smithsonian Mission Statement

For more than 160 years, the Smithsonian has remained true to its mission, "the increase and diffusion of knowledge." Today the Smithsonian is not only the world's largest provider of museum experiences supported by authoritative scholarship in science, history, and the arts but also an international leader in scientific research and exploration. The Smithsonian offers the world a picture of America, and America a picture of the world.

Special thanks to Don E. Wilson, Senior Scientist, National Museum of Natural History, Smithsonian Institution, for his invaluable contribution to this book.

This book was created by **jacob packaged goods LLC** (www.jpgglobal.com)
Written by: Melissa Stewart
Creative: Ellen Jacob, Kirk Cheyfitz, Sherry Williams, Carolyn Jackson, Dawn Camner

Photo Credits: Title page: © Barbara Gerlach/Dembinsky Photo Assoc.; **contents**: bottom left: © Wendy Dennis/Dembinsky Photo Assoc.; top right: © British Antarctic Survey/Photo Researchers, Inc.; **pages 4–5**: © Mark J. Thomas/Dembinsky Photo Assoc.; **page 5, inset**: © Alan G. Nelson/Dembinsky Photo Assoc.; **page 6**: Fred Bruemmer/Still Pictures; **page 7**: © Mark Carwardine/markcarwardine.com; **pages 8–9**: © Merlin Tuttle/Photo Researchers, Inc.; **page 9, inset**: C. Bento © Australian Museum; **page 10**: © Doug Locke/Dembinsky Photo Assoc.; **page 11**: © Anup Shah/Dembinsky Photo Assoc.; **pages 12–13**: © Alex Kerstitch/Visuals Unlimited; **page 13, inset**: © Fritz Polking/Dembinsky Photo Assoc.; **pages 14–15**: © Anthony Mercieca/Dembinsky Photo Assoc.; **page 16**: © Marilyn and Maris Kazmers/Dembinsky Photo Assoc.; **page 17**: © Barbara Gerlach/Dembinsky Photo Assoc.; **pages 18–19**: © Mark J. Thomas/Dembinsky Photo Assoc.; **page 19, inset**: © E. R. Degginger/Dembinsky Photo Assoc.; **page 20**: © Peter Parks/imagequestmarine.com; **page 21**: © Gary Meszaros/Dembinsky Photo Assoc.; **page 22**: © Kat Bolstad; **page 23**: © Mark J. Thomas/Dembinsky Photo Assoc.; **pages 24–25**: © Kjell Sandved/Visuals Unlimited; **page 26**: © Hal Horwitz/Dembinsky Photo Assoc.; **page 27**: Charles Fisher, featured in Boetius A (2005) Microfauna-Macrofauna Interaction in the Seafloor: Lessons from the Tubeworm. PLoS Biol 3(3): e102; **pages 28–29**: © Peter Batson/imagequestmarine.com; **page 29, inset**: © A. B. Sheldon/Dembinsky Photo Assoc.; **page 30**: © Ken Lucas/Visuals Unlimited; **page 31**: © Rob and Ann Simpson/Visuals Unlimited; **pages 32–33**: © Gary Meszaros/Dembinsky Photo Assoc.; **page 33, inset**: © Matthew R. Gilligan; **page 34, inset**: © Wendy Dennis/Dembinsky Photo Assoc.; **pages 34–35**: © Gouichi Wada/Nature Production/Auscape; **page 36**: © British Antarctic Survey/Photo Researchers, Inc.; **page 37**: J. M. Storey, Carleton University; **page 38**: © Barbara Gerlach/Dembinsky Photo Assoc.; **page 39**: © Fritz Polking/Dembinsky Photo Assoc.; **page 40**: © Gary Meszaros/Dembinsky Photo Assoc.; **page 41**: © Ingo Arndt/Naturepl.com; **page 42**: © Oliver Meckes and Nicole Ottawa/Photo Researchers, Inc.; **page 43**: © Barbara Gerlach/Dembinsky Photo Assoc.; **page 45**: bottom left: © Fritz Polking/Dembinsky Photo Assoc.; **page 46**: J. M. Storey, Carleton University; **page 47**: © Barbara Gerlach/Dembinsky Photo Assoc.

contents

How do different living things share Earth?

Think of ants and apple trees, mushrooms and monkeys, cats and condors.

Ants live all over the world and eat almost anything you can think of.

Millions of **species**, or kinds, of living things share our world. They live in many different places, and they get food in a variety of ways. They have different ways of staying safe and different ways of raising their young. Each species has its own special way of living and growing. This is how all living things can survive on Earth at the same time.

Compared to people, some living things seem very large or very small. Others seem very fast or very slow. Some seem to live a long time. Others seem to have a large number of babies each year.

Condors are scavengers.

Even though the way a creature looks or the way it lives may seem strange to us, every living thing is perfectly suited to survive in its **habitat**.

What is the LARGEST living thing?

Think of the largest creature you've ever seen. Was it an elephant? Maybe it was a tree. The largest creature on Earth is much harder to spot. It's not a plant or an animal. It's a fungus.

The world's largest honey fungus lives below an Oregon forest. It's been growing underground for at least 2,400 years.

The fungus is more than three miles across in some places. It's so big, no **predator** could possibly eat the entire fungus.

How does the honey fungus get its food? It sends out shoots that steal water and **nutrients** from trees. It also breaks down dead material and then returns some of the nutrients to the soil.

Most of a honey fungus's body is underground. Once a year, it produces mushrooms that help it reproduce.

Because blue whales are so big, they have no natural enemies.

What is the LARGEST living animal?

Compared to the honey fungus, the blue whale isn't that big. But it is far and away the largest living animal on Earth. An average blue whale is longer than two school buses placed end to end. And at 187 tons, the giant **mammal** weighs as much as 30 very large elephants.

Blue whales are so large that they have no natural enemies. They eat tiny shrimplike creatures called krill. Each day, a blue whale strains more than three tons of these little animals out of the ocean water that passes through its mouth.

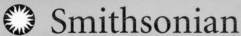

What are the smallest living things?

The world is full of tiny living things.

The bumblebee bat is one of the rarest bats in the world.

The smallest creatures on Earth are bacteria. Made up of just a single cell, most bacteria are so tiny that you can see them only through a microscope.

The smallest fish (and the smallest living creature with a backbone) is the stout infantfish. At less than one third of an inch long, it could easily sit on top of a pencil eraser. This tiny fish lives off the coast of Australia. For its small size, it has a large mouth and eats even tinier creatures called plankton.

The Jaragua gecko isn't much larger than an infantfish. From the tip of its nose to the base of its tail, this little lizard is about half the width of a dime. It eats insects. When it senses danger, it hides in cracks in tree bark.

The bumblebee bat is just over an inch long, making it the world's smallest mammal. It sleeps all day long. At night, it hunts for flies.

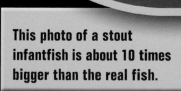

This photo of a stout infantfish is about 10 times bigger than the real fish.

SMITHSONIAN LINK
Read about these tiny creatures at Bat Facts, found in the Small Mammals section of the National Zoo online.
http://nationalzoo.si.edu/animals/smallmammals/fact-bats.cfm

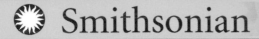

What is the **tallest** living thing?

Think of the tallest living thing in your neighborhood. It's probably a tree. Like all plants, trees use energy from the sun to make food. The tallest trees can take in the most sunlight. Being tall really helps a tree get the nutrients it needs.

The tallest tree in the world is a giant redwood called Stratosphere Giant. It lives in a California forest. The 370-foot-tall tree rises higher than a 40-story building.

Like Stratosphere Giant, most of the world's tallest trees live in Humboldt Redwoods State Park in California.

What is the tallest animal?

Y ou probably already know the answer to this question. It's the giraffe. Male giraffes can grow up to 18 feet tall. That's three times taller than most adult men. Using its long tongue, a giraffe can easily grab leaves and twigs that other animals can't reach. A giraffe's height also helps it spot enemies before they can get too close.

Giraffes use their tough lips and long tongues to strip leaves off thorny acacia trees.

What is the *FASTEST* animal?

This is a difficult question to answer. Different animals move in different ways. Some swim. Others fly or run. The cheetah is the world's fastest runner.

Sailfish can swim at top speed for long periods of time.

This big African cat can reach a top speed of 64 miles per hour, but not for long. After just 20 seconds, a cheetah must slow down.

Sailfish live in warm ocean waters around the world. They can cruise through the water at up to 68 miles per hour. That's faster than the speed limit on many highways. A sailfish's super speed helps it chase down smaller fish and other ocean animals. Scientists think its back fin, or "sail," helps it make sharp turns.

When a peregrine falcon spots a potential meal, it can hurl through the air at more than 200 miles per hour. That makes it the fastest bird—and the fastest animal—on Earth. With speed like that, it's no surprise that a peregrine falcon usually catches its **prey**.

Cheetahs can sprint for only a few seconds.

The speed of a sailfish and a cheetah is nothing compared to the diving speed of a peregrine falcon, a bird of prey found on every continent except Antarctica.

SMITHSONIAN LINK
Watch a real live cheetah, right now! Just click on the Cheetah Cam (under Live Animal Cams) at the National Zoo online.
http://nationalzoo.si.edu/animals/africansavanna/default.cfm

Brown-throated three-toed sloths live in the tropical forests of Central and South America, where they sleep up to 20 hours a day. The rest of the time, they hang upside down and slowly feed on nearby leaves. Because sloths sleep so much and move so slowly, they don't have to eat as much food as other animals their size.

Sloths **digest** food the same way they do everything else—very slowly. People usually digest their food in about a day. It may take sloths more than a month.

Think about how many times you go to the bathroom every day. A sloth gets rid of its wastes only once a week. It climbs slowly to the ground, digs a hole, and buries up to 2 pounds of dung. That's a lot of waste for an animal that may weigh only 10 pounds!

Just how slow are sloths? They may take six hours to travel just one mile. That's about 10 times slower than a person might stroll down a beach.

What is the slowest mammal?

Not all animals need speed to survive.

A sloth doesn't have to run from its enemies. As long as it stays perfectly still, it blends into its forest surroundings.

Which animal swims the **farthest** each year?

Gray whales can swim up to 9,900 miles a year. These whales **migrate** between two different homes. Each spring, they travel to their summer feeding grounds off the coast of Alaska. In autumn, they swim south to the waters off Mexico. During the winter, the whales mate and raise their young.

In the 1930s, gray whales were almost extinct. Now that they are protected by laws, more than 26,000 live in Earth's oceans.

Which animal flies the farthest each year?

The arctic tern holds the world's record for longest migration.

In April or May, arctic terns travel to an area near the North Pole. All summer long, they feed on insects and fish. They also mate and raise their young.

In September or October, the birds fly all the way to Antarctica. While it is freezing cold in their northern home, the terns enjoy the southern summer. They spend the long, sunny days feeding on fish and tiny ocean creatures.

SMITHSONIAN LINK
Learn more about the different types of birds on the Birds page at the National Zoo online.
http://nationalzoo.si.edu/animals/birds/

Some arctic terns migrate as far as 18,600 miles each year.

The arctic tern migrates almost twice as far as a gray whale.

What are the **STRONGEST** creatures?

The blue whale (see page 7) may be the largest and heaviest animal in the world. But that doesn't mean it's the strongest.

Elephants can lift hundreds of pounds, but some insects are stronger for their size.

The African savanna elephant is the heaviest animal on land. A full-grown male elephant can weigh as much as 12 tons, or 24,000 pounds. It could easily carry all the kids in your class—plus your teacher. That's pretty strong!

But for its size, the rhinoceros beetle is even stronger. Scientists have shown that these little insects can carry up to 100 times their body weight. Some people claim they can lift even more.

In the wild, rhinoceros beetles don't normally carry heavy loads, but their super strength comes in handy as they battle rivals for mates. It also helps them bulldoze their way across the forest floor in search of food and dig burrows to escape from enemies.

Rhinoceros beetles can lift 100 times their body weight.

Sometimes a creature's most extreme feature can help it in many different ways.

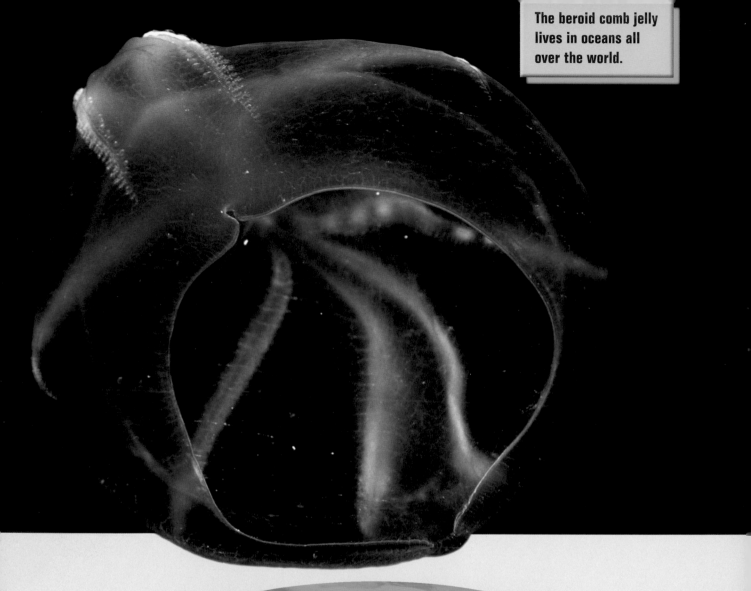

Which animal has the largest MOUTH?

Has anyone ever called you a big mouth? Compared to your body, your mouth really isn't very big. Take a look at a beroid comb jelly. It's mostly mouth and stomach. With such a gigantic mouth, it can eat most prey whole.

Which animal has the LONGEST tongue?

The Morgan's Madagascan sphinx moth has a 14-inch tongue. That's pretty amazing for an insect less than 2 inches long. The moth uses its long tongue to reach the sugary **nectar** deep inside the comet orchids that grow in the forests of Madagascar. (That's an island off the coast of Africa.)

Scientists first saw the Morgan's Madagascan sphinx moth in 1903.

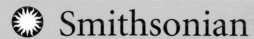
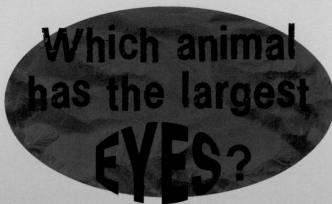
Which animal has the largest EYES?

Colossal squids live in deep ocean areas near Antarctica.

They are some of the strangest animals in the world. Their bodies glow in the dark, and they can grow up to 49 feet long.

This squid's most amazing feature is its huge eyes. They are more than 2 feet wide.

SMITHSONIAN LINK
Read more facts about undersea creatures on the Ocean Living page at the National Zoo online.
http://nationalzoo.si.edu/animals/oceanliving/facts/default.cfm

The colossal squid is the world's largest animal without a backbone.

Colossal squids probably use their giant eyes to spot prey. (Model shown in photo.)

Mantis shrimps use their amazing strength to punch holes through the shells of their prey.

Which animal can see the **most** colors?

Mantis shrimps live in shallow ocean waters all over the world. Their eyes are mounted on stalks that can swivel in any direction. They can also see colors you can't even imagine. People can see about 10,000 different colors, but mantis shrimps may be able to see a million.

Most coral-reef predators have trouble spotting shellfish. But mantis shrimps can easily see their prey in their colorful coral-reef home.

Which plant has the **LARGEST** flower?

Most plants produce many flowers each year, but the rafflesia is different. Each plant produces one enormous flower. It can grow up to 3 feet across and weigh as much as 25 pounds. Now that's big!

The rafflesia grows in the rain forests of Southeast Asia. Its huge size and strong smell make it easy for beetles and flies to find. When they arrive, they drink the flower's nectar and spread its **pollen**. Then the plant makes thousands of tiny seeds, and some grow into new plants.

Which plant has the **LARGEST** seeds?

Another amazing plant is the coco-de-mer palm. The seeds of this plant can be up to 19 inches across and weigh more than 48 pounds.

Why are the seeds so huge? That's a question no one can answer. We do know that the coco-de-mer palm is in no hurry to grow. It takes 9 months for its first leaf to grow. And the first flowers may not appear for 60 years.

It grows only in the Seychelle Islands in the Indian Ocean.

This flower is the only part of the rafflesia you'll ever see. The plant has no leaves or stems. Its tiny roots grow inside a tropical vine.

Which plant has the LONGEST life?

The oldest tree in California may be a bristlecone pine that has survived for more than 4,000 years. Even though large parts of the tree's trunk are now dead, it still produces seeds every year.

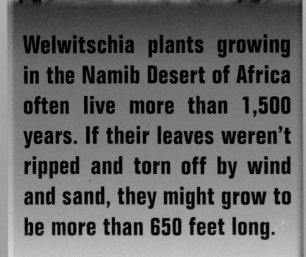

Welwitschia plants growing in the Namib Desert of Africa often live more than 1,500 years. If their leaves weren't ripped and torn off by wind and sand, they might grow to be more than 650 feet long.

This bristlecone pine was alive when the ancient Egyptians were building the pyramids.

These deep-sea tube worms grow less than one half inch each year.

Which animal has the LONGEST life?

If you are lucky, you may live to be 100 years old. Some tortoises and whales can live even longer. But the world's oldest animals are six-foot-tall tube worms living in the Gulf of Mexico. Scientists think they are at least 250 years old. That means they were alive during the American Revolutionary War.

SMITHSONIAN LINK
There are more invertebrates than you think! Learn about them at the National Zoo online's Invertebrates page.
http://nationalzoo.si.edu/animals/invertebrates/facts/default.cfm

Smithsonian

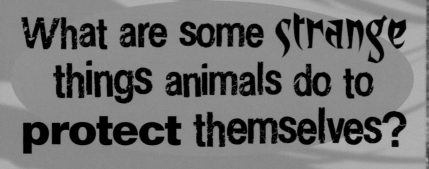

What are some strange things animals do to protect themselves?

Because living things eat one another to survive, creatures must have ways to protect themselves from enemies.

A hagfish swims into its prey's body and tears the victim to bits from the inside out.

Some animals run away. Others try to hide. Still others smell bad or act in frightening ways.

When a Texas horned lizard senses danger, it freezes in place. Its coloring helps it blend in with its surroundings.

If a bird gets too close, the lizard hisses fiercely. If a snake attacks, the lizard pierces its enemy with its horns and spines. If a coyote or fox is nearby, the lizard squirts blood from openings behind its eyes.

The hagfish looks like an eel and lives on the ocean bottom in cold waters. When a hagfish is attacked, it quickly produces a thick slime. The sticky goo mixes with seawater and spreads out to surround the predator. The enemy can't escape, and it can't breathe. The hagfish swims to safety. The predator usually dies.

A Texas horned lizard eat lots of ants —more than 200 a day.

Scientists discovered golden poison dart frogs in 1978, but native peoples have used their poison for hundreds of years.

What is the most poisonous animal?

The tiny golden poison dart frog uses brightly colored skin as a warning to enemies living in the rain forests of South America.

When a bird or lizard chomps down on a golden poison dart frog, it gets a big surprise. The frog's skin is deadly to the touch. The skin of one frog contains enough poison to kill 100 people.

Some animals run away from predators. Others jump or glide, fly or hide.

What is the most poisonous plant?

Plants can't run and they can't hide. That means they're easy to find and eat. To protect themselves from hungry insects and other animals, many plants produce poisonous chemicals.

The most dangerous chemicals are found in the castor-oil plant. Eating just one castor bean seed can cause a slow, painful death.

Oil from castor beans is used to make soap, candles, crayons, and other products.

Which plant eats insects?

Most animals can run or swim or fly around to look for food. But plants spend their whole lives stuck in one spot. They can't grow unless they get energy from the sun and minerals from the soil.

The Venus flytrap grows in wetlands, where the soil doesn't have many minerals. How does this plant get the food it needs? When an insect lands on its leaves, they suddenly snap shut. The insect is trapped inside. Then special chemicals slowly digest the insect's body.

It takes a Venus flytrap about a week to digest an insect.

Which animal lives in another animal's MOUTH?

When is a tongue not really a tongue? When it's an isopod—a small, shrimplike creature. Some isopods cruise the ocean waters in search of spotted rose snapper fish. When they find one, they grab onto the fish's tongue and gobble it up. Then they hook themselves to the back of the fish's mouth and take the tongue's place. Life is good in their new home. They are safe from predators and can steal bits of food every time the fish eats.

This isopod is the only creature known to replace the body organ of another animal.

The spittlebug is a plant-sucking insect. When it senses danger, it jumps up with great speed and force. This insect's powerful back legs push it forward with a force equal to 400 times its body weight. If one jumped in your face, it would really hurt.

The Japanese flying squirrel can't actually fly. When it jumps out of a tree and spreads its legs wide, flaps of skin catch the breeze. Gliding through the forest is much safer than scurrying along the ground.

Aardvarks can't jump or glide. They use their long claws and strong legs to dig underground tunnels. They can dig faster than two men with shovels. During the day, aardvarks sleep in their tunnels. At night, they come out to hunt for ants and termites. If a predator gets too close, they dash into a tunnel.

The Japanese flying squirrel can travel more than 360 feet in a single glide.

An aardvark's large ears and sensitive nose help it find food and avoid enemies.

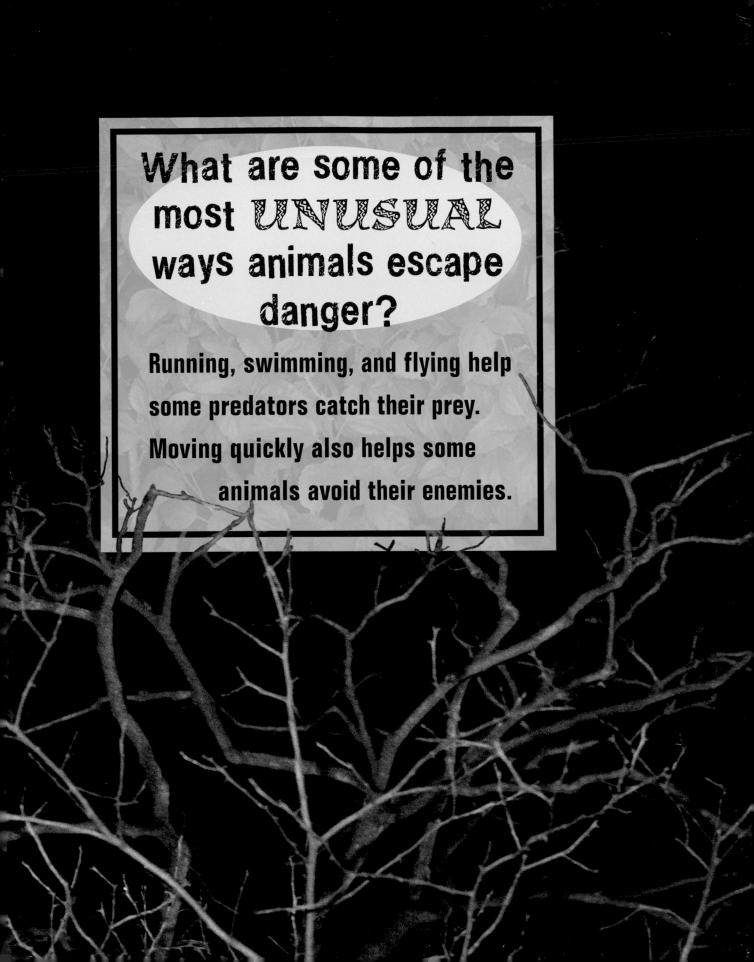

What are some of the most UNUSUAL ways animals escape danger?

Running, swimming, and flying help some predators catch their prey. Moving quickly also helps some animals avoid their enemies.

Scientists discovered these deep-sea amphipods in 1995.

Which animal lives in the deepest part of the ocean?

Living things can survive in all kinds of places. Some amphipods, tiny shrimplike creatures, make their home in the Mariana Trench. It is the deepest, darkest, and coldest part of the ocean—almost seven miles below the surface. Amphipods do just fine in these extreme conditions. They survive by eating the "marine snow," tiny bits of dead animals that drift down from above.

How do animals stay warm in **extremely** cold places?

Wood frogs can live as far north as Alaska and Canada. Each winter, they freeze solid for weeks or even months. Their hearts stop beating, and their brains stop working. They seem almost dead. But when warm weather returns, the frogs thaw out and spring back to life.

Sea otters also live in very cold places. They spend most of the day swimming in chilly ocean waters. How do they stay warm and dry? They have the thickest fur of any animal. A sea otter's short, fluffy undercoat traps warm air close to its skin. The guard hairs on top keep water away from the otter's skin.

Wood frogs are comfortable on ice. Up to one third of their body fluids can freeze without harming the frogs.

A female ostrich never leaves her eggs, even if a predator is nearby.

Which bird lays the LARGEST eggs?

Most plants start life as a seed, but most animals start life as an egg. Ostriches lay the largest eggs in the world. These giant birds can weigh up to 400 pounds, and their eggs can weigh as much as 39 pounds.

Brown kiwi eggs are much smaller than ostrich eggs. They weigh only about a pound. But brown kiwi eggs are huge compared to the birds that lay them. A female brown kiwi weighs only about 6 pounds.

SMITHSONIAN LINK
Read about the future of the ostrich and other birds in the *Zoogoer* magazine found at the National Zoo online.
http://nationalzoo.si.edu/publications/zoogoer/2004/3/birds.cfm

Which bird sits on its eggs the LONGEST?

The male emperor penguin sits on his mate's egg through the long, cold Antarctic winter. It may take 67 days for the egg to hatch, but the father penguin never leaves. No other bird works so hard to keep its eggs warm.

A brown kiwi usually lays two or three eggs a year. It takes up to 84 days for each one to hatch. So it's a good thing male kiwis take turns sitting on the eggs.

A male emperor penguin holds a chick on top of his feet so it won't touch the cold snow.

Which animal produces the MOST young?

Aphids produce young without mating. They can give birth up to 10 times in a single summer. Their young produce more aphids in the same way. So one aphid can start a chain that creates a billion new insects in just one year.

Aphids are tiny insects that suck sugary juices out of plants all summer long.

A hungry ladybug can eat more than 200 aphids in a single day.

Alpine salamanders live in the mountain forests of Europe.

Which animal is pregnant the LONGEST?

Some animals give birth to fully formed babies. It takes human babies about 9 months to grow and develop. Mice are pregnant for just a few weeks. Elephants carry their young for about 22 months. But that's not the world's record.

The alpine salamander may carry its young for more than 3 years. These little salamanders live on damp, cold mountaintops. Summers are short, and winters are long. It takes many months for mother salamanders to find all the food their young need to grow and develop. Carrying the little ones for a long time helps insure that more of them survive.

What is the most numerous animal on Earth?

The most numerous creatures on Earth can live in many different kinds of habitats, from the Arctic to the tropics. They eat many kinds of food, produce many young, and know how to stay safe from predators.

What animal does all these things well? A tiny worm called the nematode. An acre of rich soil may contain 3 billion nematodes. They can also live in lakes and oceans. They can even live inside people and other animals.

This photo of a nematode was taken through a microscope and magnified more than 1,000 times.

What are the RAREST animals on Earth?

Most animals are not nearly as common as nematodes. Many large animals are becoming less numerous all the time. As people destroy the natural homes of gorillas, rhinoceroses, and elephants, it gets harder and harder for these animals to survive.

Giant tortoises are among the rarest animals in the world. Today they live on just a few tropical islands. Yangtze River dolphins and ivory-billed woodpeckers are also in danger of disappearing from Earth forever. Only by working together can we save the precious creatures that share our world.

Because giant tortoises taste delicious, most of them have been killed for food. Very few are left on Earth today.

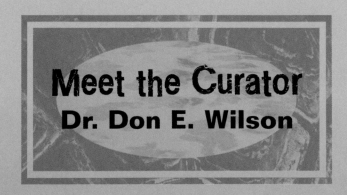

Meet the Curator
Dr. Don E. Wilson

Why did you become a scientist?

When I was in college, I discovered a natural affinity for classes in natural history. I loved the fieldwork associated with them, and after getting my degree in wildlife management, I knew that I wanted to go to graduate school and get a Ph.D. in biology so that I could spend my career doing research on plants and animals.

Did anything or anyone from your childhood influence your decision?

As a child, I had an abiding curiosity about the natural world. My father was an outdoorsman, and he took me with him on many hunting and fishing trips. I loved hunting and fishing, and collecting things in general.

What would you most like to discover in your field of science?

As a systematic mammalogist, I am mainly concerned with the classification of mam-

mals. Part of that involves the discovery of new species of mammals, and those kinds of discoveries, based on fieldwork, are still the most exciting to me.

What is the most important unanswered question in your field?

I just published a book called *Mammal Species of the World*. It is the third edition of this work. Each edition has been a more complete attempt at classifying all the world's mammal species. Understanding all the evolutionary relationships of mammals is the goal of such studies, and although we make increasingly great progress each year, the end is still not in sight. If we did understand the complete history of our gene pool, it would open the way to amazing new discoveries.

What do you do on a daily basis?

Now I spend most of my time sitting at the computer in my office, writing and corresponding with colleagues around the world. In this new electronic age, it is possible to be connected instantly with people working virtually anywhere in the world. However, I am still surrounded by my library of published literature on mammals, and I constantly consult works published as long ago as 1758, when the scientist Carl Linnaeus published the first scientifically accurate catalog of life on Earth.

Where and when do you do your research?

I do much of my research right here in the National Museum of Natural History as well as in other natural history museums. These collections are a priceless resource for understanding the natural world and our place in it. I also do fieldwork collecting and studying mammals. I specialize in bats, and my studies have led me to every continent and almost a hundred countries.

What do you like most about your job?

The thrill of discovery never dulls, whether I'm out in the field collecting a specimen of a bat that I have never seen before, or I'm poring over a dusty volume in the library. I get up at 4 A.M. every morning and can't wait to get to work and learn something new and different each day.

What do you like least about your job?

As part of a large organization, I have to attend meetings and complete paperwork for a variety of things that have little to do with my scientific research. Those minor frustrations are a small price to pay for the opportunity to do exactly what I love to do.

Glossary

digest—to break down food into nutrients the body can use for energy

habitat—the place where a living thing usually can be found

mammal—an animal that has a backbone, is warm-blooded, and feeds its young with its mother's milk. All have hair or fur, but many marine mammals, which live mostly or completely in the water, have lost much of their hair

migrate—to travel a long distance to find food or a place to mate and raise young

nectar—a sugary liquid many flowers produce to attract insects and animals so that they can spread the plant's pollen

nutrient—a substance that provides a living thing with elements it needs to live and grow

pollen—powdery spores that must be transferred to the female part of a flower to make a seed

predator—an animal that kills and eats other animals

prey—an animal that is hunted and killed by another animal for food

species—a group of similar creatures that can mate and produce healthy young

Places to Visit

Websites

www.extremescience.com/creatport.htm
World Records of the Animal Kingdom

http://waynesword.palomar.edu/ww0601.htm
Amazing Trivia about Plants

http://nationalzoo.si.edu/
Learn more about the variety of different species
at the Smithsonian National Zoo online.

http://nationalzoo.si.edu/animals/animalrecords/
Like good trivia? Check out more animal records, even the deadliest animal
(hint: it is not what you'd expect) at the Animal Records page on the National Zoo online.

http://nationalzoo.si.edu/animals/asianelephants/
Check out the live Elephant Cam at the National Zoo online.

http://nationalzoo.si.edu/animals/reptilesamphibians/
Read fun facts about reptiles at the Reptiles and Amphibians Fact Sheet at the National Zoo online.

**There are links to many wonderful web pages in this book. But the web is constantly growing
and changing and we cannot guarantee that the sites we recommend will be available. If the site
you want is no longer there, you can always find your way to plenty of information about nature
and a great learning experience through the main Smithsonian website: www.si.edu.**

Suggested Reading

Almost Gone: The World's Rarest Animals, by Steve Jenkins.

Amazing Animals: Nature's Most Incredible Creatures, by Sneed Collard
and Anthony D. Fredericks.

Freaky Flowers, by D. M. Souza.

How a Seed Grows, by Helene J. Jordan.

The Outrageous Animal Record Book, by Joanne Mattern.

What Color Is Camouflage?, by Carolyn B. Otto.

Index